T0130514

The Hotel Haikus

TS Hawkins & T. McLean

iUniverse, Inc.
Bloomington

The Hotel Haikus

First printed by Wordclay on November 15, 2012
Cover Design by Rebecca Gissel
Haiku definition by Dictionary.com

iUniverse books may be ordered through booksellers or by contacting:

iUniverse
1663 Liberty Drive
Bloomington, IN 47403
www.iuniverse.com
1-800-Authors (1-800-288-4677)

ISBN: 978-1-4759-7589-5 (sc)
ISBN: 978-1-4759-7590-1 (e)

Printed in the United States of America

iUniverse rev. date: 02/05/2013

The Hotel Haikus

TS Hawkins & T. McLean

haiku: a major form of Japanese verse, written in seventeen syllables divided into three lines of five, seven, five and employing highly evocative allusions and comparisons often on the subject of nature or one of the seasons *haiku*: a major form of Japanese verse, written in seventeen syllables divided into three lines of five, seven, five and employing highly evocative allusions and comparisons often on the subject of nature or one of the seasons *haiku*: a major form of Japanese verse, written in seventeen syllables divided into three lines of five, seven, five and employing highly evocative allusions and comparisons often on the subject of nature or one of the seasons *haiku*: a major form of Japanese verse, written in seventeen syllables divided into three lines of five, seven, five and employing highly evocative allusions and comparisons often on the subject of nature or one of the seasons *haiku*: a major form of Japanese verse, written in seventeen syllables divided into three lines of five, seven, five and employing highly evocative allusions and comparisons often on the subject of nature or one of the seasons

The Hotel Haikus

haiku: a major form of Japanese verse, written in seventeen syllables divided into three lines of five, seven, five and employing highly evocative allusions and comparisons often on the subject of nature or one of the seasons *haiku*: a major form of Japanese verse, written in seventeen syllables divided into three lines of five, seven, five and employing highly evocative allusions and comparisons often on the subject of nature or one of the seasons *haiku*: a major form of Japanese verse, written in seventeen syllables divided into three lines of five, seven, five and employing highly evocative allusions and comparisons often on the subject of nature or one of the seasons *haiku*: a major form of Japanese verse, written in seventeen syllables divided into three lines of five, seven, five and employing highly evocative allusions and comparisons often on the subject of nature or one of the seasons *haiku*: a major form of Japanese verse, written in seventeen syllables divided into three lines of five, seven, five and employing highly evocative allusions and comparisons often on the subject of nature or one of the seasons seventeen syllables divided into three lines of five, seven, five and employing highly evocative allusions and comparisons often on the subject of nature or one of the seasons *haiku*: a major form of Japanese verse, written in seventeen syllables divided into three lines of five, seven, five and employing highly evocative allusions and em

OTHER TITLES BY TS HAWKINS

***

Sugar Lumps and Black Eye Blues
Confectionately Yours
Mahogany Nectar
Lil Blæk Book: All the Long Stories Short
Running Still Water

UPCOMING RELEASES
Black Suga: diary of a troublesome teenager
Poetry Schmo-etry
A Woman Scorned is a Woman Blessed
On My Knees Too Long: Prayers, Proverbs & Poems to GOD
Becoming Saturn: Counting Backwards from 60-30

Books/CDs available for purchase at all major online retailers
&
www.tspoetics.com

OTHER TITLES BY T. MCLEAN

***

UPCOMING RELEASES
M.M.K
After the Surgery and Cigarettes
Sinful Sips of Saccharine Dreams

For more information, visit
http://saccharinedreams.blogspot.com

ACKNOWLEDGEMENTS

***

Joseph for not changing the back locks…

The mis-education of a troublesome neighborhood…

Those who came to our rescue!

Readers of *Sugar Lumps and Black Eye Blues, Confectionately Yours, Mahogany Nectar & Lil Blæk Book*

DEDICATION

***

Much love to our families & mentors

Macedonia Baptist Church

Dorothy Lewis-Hawkins

Bessie Dutton

Rudolph Lewis

Eloise Lewis

Dorothy Simmons

Eloise McLean

M Diggs

"240"

CONTENTS

***

CHECK-IN

***

Side-table notes from the Authors

"*A blessing in disguise...*" Mothers always know when to state this old adage to help the smoke settle from a child's clouded mind. Thus, this little nugget of wisdom was rendered **AFTER** she hung the phone up on me when I called to relay the news that my apartment building had been set on fire. Yes, you read correctly...set on fire! With the many diversions in my life's journey that she's blueprinted for me, nothing much jolts her as of late. To my surprise, when I phoned home to convey that evening's happenings, she was more equipped to deal with the possibility that I had been hit by a car because I was texting and walking while crossing the street rather than the news I had to ultimately deliver. Apparently, the fire was the hook and knife in her parental footing launching a deepen notch in her belt of worry. This worry resulted in her panicking and hanging up the phone on me in time of crisis. So, after all my tears, screaming and the melee of debris to clean, this tragic event ignited some creativity [and perhaps humor for you the reader] as I pen haikus to document the ups and so many downs of this experience; *the disguised blessing*. Hopefully, this tome will serve as the phoenix for my spirit and a treasure trove for your leisure afternoon. Happy reading!

~TS Hawkins

It is with sincerest gratitude that I would like to thank everyone that took part in the creation of this work. I have been humbled tremendously by the little inspirations I've found in my daily paths that have lead up to this very moment. The small things that save my life every...single...day. The joy of my mother's laughter; the timbre of my father's voice; the strength in my aunt; the passion of my grandparents or the guidance of my mentor, I've had a safe place in all of you. You inspire me to be better than I was yesterday and I am forever indebted to you. I would like to dedicate this book to my grandmothers for their constant belief in me. May their undoubting souls rest peacefully with their savior. Together they have taught me perseverance, patience and passion in everything that I do. In moments that I can't see the road ahead of me, their words linger in my spirit and I smile. Somehow, I know they're smiling right back at me! Thank you so much ☺

~T. McLean

CONCIERGE MESSAGE

***

"ON LOW SIMMER"
a preface by Dr. Kimmika L. H. Williams-Witherspoon

(Referencing the old, ambiguous "they"), they say, that *"Necessity is the mother of invention"*...or, is it, *"Good things come out of adversity"?* I forget.

Either way, on December 13, 2011, a fire alarm rang out at an apartment building at 1615 W. Westmoreland St. (behind the Temple University Medical School). Following the swift response of the Philadelphia Fire Department, 3 rental units/three "families" found themselves, all of a sudden and with little warning or preparation, displaced, homeless, in need of the Red Cross and in want of emergency care.

Relocated to hotels, poets TS Hawkins and T. McLean spent 12 weeks clinging to the slight hope that their lives would someday go back to normal—normal, that is, minus the loss of clothing, computer, photos and personal mementos that were burned, charred or destroyed in a flash. This book, **The Hotel Haikus**, born out of those first moments, days, weeks into months of painful mourning, grieving and exploration forces the reader to critically think about what it means to be "at home" and in "safe space."

Some of the haikus included in this collection are irregular—not strictly following the three-line 5/7/5 syllable format made popular in traditional Japanese Haiku form. Some of the haiku like Hawkins' Haiku #36 are short and cryptic demanding from its readers, active participation to decode its meaning.

"Boil in ecstasy
garnish over pilaf, serve
her silver plated
--keep my outpourings in—"(p. 22)

Others, Like McLean's Haiku #5 read like abridged narratives of modern tragedy.

"Dying was supposed
to be easy, but I still
feel my thoughts burning." (p. 15)

These very *American*, urban haiku—or "poem-ku's" --vacillate between visceral, prophetic, poignant and uplifting. These pieces read like "poetic tweets" that can quickly become catchy mantra. In times of trouble, clearly, as evidenced by Hawkins and McLean's work, writing poetry--no matter how short-- or keeping a journal can keep one sane.

TS #96
Any moment can
Change the moment before it...
Always be prepared. (p. 34)

McLean #42

Humbling moments
Come too close in happenstance
Slow time so I breathe. (p. 23)

At times, between the pains of loss, the text also smacks of "laugh out loud" irony as in TS #53:

Desperate times call for
Desperate measures but DON'T
Use my underwear! (p. 25)

Or TS #59:

Hotel gym only
Has a treadmill. Mockery
Of my current life. (p. 25)

And let's not forget T. McLean's dry humor in Haiku #39, that can't help but make you smile:

"This is not the type
Of establishment I would
Choose to meet DEATH in..." (p.22)

Under extreme duress, burned out of house and home, insurance, legal woes and all the bureaucracy that goes along with reconstructing one's life, they put pen to paper and chiseled their journey the only way they knew how. Here is ethnography in *Haiku*. This book is testament that fire and tragedy cannot burn it all. Sometimes, in life, things will just "simmer"; but our laconic moments must live on—as "markers" for those of us who might pass this way.

CHAPTER I

Lobbying for Comfort

1

"Let me out here, please"
"Would you like to add a tip?" *"Yes...*
drive faster next time!"

2

Red, the only birr
audible as ninja fire-
fighters hose down hope.

3

Intensified fear;
Flames doused only by shear rage
What is happening?

4

Righteousness absent.
Flames drenched my security.
Fear settles smoothly.

5

Dying was supposed
to be easy, but I still
feel my thoughts burning.

6

Flashing darkness in
my mind; true purgatory.
Trying to escape.

7

Dubious efforts
to uphold notions of re-
fuge, charred your façade.

8

This structure is hol-
low. There is nothing left here
but bitter dreams and

loneliness left out
to dry and rot like bad news
that came way too soon

9

Mildew and mold grew
where I thought I once knew how
to live peacefully

10

Janice had a big
ole butt, but why were those the
first words he uttered
...to me...

11

Silence broke by
"Janice got a big ole butt"
haziness shattered.

12

Reality calms
Fire still burns in pieces
of what was once, you

drowning silently
in overwhelming fear of
these unknown spaces

grasping for some kind
of familiarity.
Reality's gone

Can't break free of these
nightmares around my neck, please...
Asphyxiating

Erotically
is still considered slow death,

losing parts of me

Just want to be free
Let go of me, please. Her screams
waken me *"water"*

13
Bare and broken in
½ the time it took to burn
what used to be home

14
White noise, white noise, white
noise, white noise, white noise, white noise
"Shut her the hell up"
[night #1]

15
Drowned in my solace
while she lay three feet away
Souls,   six
         feet
         under

16
Slow movements leading
quickly into afterthoughts
of my misfortune

17
A fiery pit
of watered down dreams and jokes
that became too real

18
This TV only
has four channels, which two of
them are parental

19

controlled. So once un-
locked, blast naked moans to sink
what's left of feeling.

19
Divinity show
yourself to me. Simply prove
your existence, NOW!

20
Price of luxury
is split in half, but today
no tag on safety

21
I always wondered
what it would be like to live
in a hotel room…

Be careful what you
wish for. Dreams come true just not
the way you planned it

22
Nothings esculent;
these fast paced by-products are
masking food for thought

23
Yup, she sure did just
hang the phone up on me. She's
shocked?! But I'm homeless…
            ::sigh:: "mothers"

24
He says *"Daddy, I'm
scared."* I remain silent
Sentiments the same

No father to cleave
unto; mutual in mind,
we weep until night…

25
"You are so stupid"
was all I could say. Parents
just don't understand

26
Now, having a pure
conniption. Being thrown in
to the bowels of

uncertainty. Col-
lege didn't prepare me
for those who don't go.

27
Education is
the litmus test to see who
survives in boundaries

28
Joy cometh in the
morn time. Folks miss the blessing
Sorrow kept them up

late the night before.
Someone please sound the alarm;
want to feel relief

29
Leave me here alone
to find myself in the dark-
ness of light. br_ok^en

30

No matter how hard
I try, altiloquent words
won't liquid down flames

31
I wanted to laugh
But there is nothing funny
about ignorance…

32
My high school always
celebrated success with
bonfires. Then, the

blaze made much more sense.
Flickering yellow and red
feel sad to me now

33
Humorous, Silly
and Hope are words that one day
Will make me grin…
…again

CHAPTER II

Room Service

34
I just want to have
butt naked wild monkey sex!
truest words spoken

35
Intimate outbursts
through walls not thick enough to
protect our insides

36
"Boil in ecstasy
garnish over pilaf, serve
her silver plated"
      --keep my outpourings in--

37
No one showers that
long. Know what you are doing…
Buy new soap bar, please!

38
This hotel bar is
deep fried in nothing of home.
Hunger for comfort

begins in stomach
pangs. Clicking heels I realize
was starved before now…

39
This is not the type
of establishment I would

choose to meet **DEATH** in

40
This boy is doing

HOME things!!! When will he realize
This will never be...
home?

41

The gentle sounds of
renegade lullaby blues
pacifies slowly

42

Humbling moments
come too close in happenstance
Slow time, so I breathe

43

Rings on porcelain
stained by broken promises
left on the nightstand.

44

Chestnuts roasting on
an open fire has new
meaning for me. In

the meantime, I re-
sist the urge to hang my sor-
rows in parmesan

45

Broken window panes
only tell half the story,
brimstone bowties the

rest. Flames folly present
despair, control has no place
to live here either.

Vaporous sulfur
fills space where memories sleep.

Could use an "OZ" now.

46
Why are we still here
Ike? Distorting movie quotes
passes the slow time

47
::ugh::
I came here with a
suitcase and dream. I want
my fucking suitcase.

48
Jingle bells, Batman
smells and Robin just had an
orgasm…FUCK THAT!

49
The woman next door
makes more noise than animals
feasting on food scraps

50
Wish I knew what all
these emotions meant. This grey
space is irony.

51
Sixteen channels to
show me how to die gently
in my own sorrow

52
Cartoons, like Allen
Gregory, are icebreakers
when family visits

53

What he doesn't know
is that I cry for him too
Today…break for me

54

Entrapped in the same
element of danger you
tried to break free from

55

Desperate times call for
desperate measures but DON'T
use my underwear!

56

Wanted to pick my
nose for the past hour and
a half, **"LOOK OVER THERE!"**

57

His snoring irks me!
Sibilant disdain wrapped in
someone I once liked…

58

THANK YOU TEQUILLA
THANK YOU *TEQUILLA* LOVE YOU
TEQUILLA, HUG YOU

59

Hotel gym only
has a treadmill. Mockery
of my current life

60

Housekeeping won't change
my sheets. Landlord won't pick up
phone. Nowhere to go.

CHAPTER III

Passing, Strange?

61

Hanging from rafters
is the only thought I can
muster walking home…

62

Tumultuously
finding a way to cope with
harsh realities

63

~~I am okay, I~~
~~am okay, I am okay~~
~~I am okay, I'm~~
…not…

64

Two full beds, empty
spirits into plastic cups
No saludé; just drink

65

Cold food eaten with
cold hands, reaching deeper in-
side my soul than God

66

Farted, so sorry
not embarrassed but in shared
space, it intrudes on

67

Falsified
true lies can kill you
so nicely

68

Tragedy strikes twice
Always sharp blows to egos

of devout faithfuls

69
Tried to masturbate
tonight. It's hard to compete
with the room next door…

70
Mentally moving
nowhere. Trying to keep up
with nothing left. Lost.

71
As luck would have it
got my period today
with $4 and

2 pairs of under-
wear, creativity is
sparked for 7 days

72
Home is supposed to
be where the heart is. But I
can't feel my heartbeat

73
Mind racing. My soul
will not pay the price for your
inadequacies.

74
Close quarters make for
dumb games played by tattered souls,
liver suffers most

75
Leave for work in the
morning. Old man walks in hall

for exercise but

He is still there when
I return, in the same spot
when I left for work…
[*blue-haired struggles*]

76

Tried to masturbate
again. The clack of the door
reminds me…not home!
[night #17]

77

A ruck of bad news
makes this moment sweeter than
that moschate house
::uck::

78

Want to masturbate
or at least whet my whistle!
::THIS ARRANGEMENT SUCKS::

79

If I could turn back
time, would erase the moment
your parents made you.

Obviously it
wasn't a stint well spent. You're
the fresh smell of hell.

80

Started new job in
borrowed clothes. Placate colleagues
that every things fine…

81

Laugh, laughter, laughing
Much needed release because
I cry real ugly
LOL!

82

*"Take a shot every
hour you waste on Facebook!"*
::this is not coping::

83

Dear Middle of the
Night: thank you for silent moans
lain undercover!

CHAPTER IV

Tabbing Out

84
Sometimes when you feel
you have life all figured out
it figures…screw you

85
Slowly pilfered 'til
there was nothing left to give
Almost gave my life

86
Black **people** we have
got to **do** so much **better**
…much needed mantra…

87
Stop telling me to
find the silver lining. I'm
querulous because

they burnt my home down.
There's nothing vernal about
inconsiderate

nature of piss poor,
unstable emotions from
others not my kin!

88
Pity, I don't need
What I could use is a friend,
but I see no one

89
Words limit the
frustrations of life penned in
soft whispers. Sob past

and present; fingers

wipe moistened weakness from
a future unknown

90

Room 216 sat
between 217 and
215 but I

only sat, waiting
on the ticker tape of new
news to piece me whole
[again]

91

p u s h i n g to survive
in a chaotic calmness
warring with ideals

92

Hushed reverie
is more than just lullabies
that cradle this life.
[night #34]

93

There's nothing adroit
about him. Every month paid
in full. Don't trust him…
…anymore

94

Molded memories
left on smoked glass shattered on
concrete steps to hell

95

There was no air in
Beirut. Battlefields of mice and
men in turmoil

96
Any moment can
change the moment before it…
always be prepared

97
Cleanse me. Lather me.
Scour flesh, sand down impure
feelings. Doubt no more

98
Can't organize the
insanity. So live life
moments at a time

99
Sweet serenity
in hearing the words **good-bye**
from the hotel clerk!

100
With twelve dollars and
a dream, left nothing behind to be
worried about. I

began again in
hopes that this singed pride would not
linger on spirit.

FRONT DESK REMINDER

***

"HISTORY, HEALING and HAIKU"
an afterward by Jacquelyn E. McCullough

The fire was real…feelings, reactions, needs, fear, questions, one right after another or jumbled together; all were very tangible. In this context perhaps haiku is the only way the authors were able to relate, relay or understand what happened.

"Haiku, unrhymed Japanese poetic form consisting of 17 syllables arranged in three lines of 5, 7, and 5 syllables respectively." (Encyclopedia Britannica) The Japanese write their haiku in one line, in order to see clearly the parts of the haiku. In English each part is given a line. This allows the reader time to form an image in the mind before the eyes go back to the left margin for more words. Moreover, the line breaks act as a type of punctuation. (A Lesson by Shahriyer Shuvo) It took me a long time to 'get' the haiku style reading **The Hotel Haikus**. I asked both TS Hawkins and T. McLean why this style was used. From Mr. McLean: *"Haikus are very straightforward. They strike an emotion quickly. With a haiku you don't have time to react; you just feel (much like our experience with the fire).* Haikus are very direct and give you precise insight into the poem so that you are either left wanting more, or you feel closure by the end of it. From Ms. Hawkins: *"Why haiku? With taking this horrible experience of our apartment building being set on fire and truncating the feelings into this form helps bring creative clarity to the situation. …it helps get to the root of each moment and emotion."* Emotion seems to be the root of this book. Somewhere between my 7th and 10th reading of **The Hotel Haikus** I realized that I had to let go, I had to stop forcing my reading to what I have known and allow myself to discover the unknown. When I started

reading again, I didn't so much read but drift, scan through the lines if you will. Similar to a squint so your eyes can 'see' a different view of things, I pushed aside the temptation to control the flow – to direct the haiku. Without conscious awareness, the pictures came; all the images, the feelings. Interpreting these haikus was like discovering a new way of enjoying literature. For me it has been unlike anything I have come across previously. Reading **The Hotel Haikus**, one does not enjoy a 'story', one is immersed in an event. Pictures unfold along with the reactions one might have had, had they been in the authors' situation. Mr. Mclean said it best *"Haikus are very straightforward. They strike an emotion quickly."* Once I let go, the pieces in the book flowed like water in a stream with eddies and banks sometimes slow sometimes rushing toward who knows what. Ms. Hawkins brought more understanding when she shared *"the brevity is very freeing in a way."* It is the brevity that moves you through the experience, allowing the reader to 'free' his or her mind to enjoy the ride. As someone who has always relied on the 'visual' to better comprehend the physical, I have found that this venue suits me. I can let go with haiku. I can 'feel' the emotion and thereby become a part of the haiku. Through letting go and feeling the ebb and tide of each piece, I found I could distinguish the different styles between the authors. It was a pleasant discovery since the styles augment or support or even wrap around one another in a way that reflects how one might experience something as 'in your face' as a fire. There is the immediate urgency and the emotion of a screaming mind trying to exert sanity on an insane condition while holding desperately to a civility that might break at any moment.

Shahriyer Shuvo, a haiku poet from Bangladesh explains "The kigo, or season word, is a vital part of the Japanese haiku, but in English it is often ignored and not well understood. The Japanese, because of their longer history of reading haiku, understand that there are two parts to the poem. In English these are called the phrase and

38

fragment. One line is the fragment and the other two lines combine grammatically to become the phrase. Without this combining, the two lines together in the haiku will sound 'choppy' as the voice drops at the end of each line. We understand this when reading *"Righteousness absent. Flames drenched my security. Fear settles smoothly."* (McLean) and *"Dubious efforts to uphold notions of refuge charred your façade."* (Hawkins)

The making of a haiku is a journey in and of itself; a writer could devote a life time to perfecting the style and mastering the sine qua non in of the poem. These authors have managed to create their own style that compliments the historical origin of haiku. If this is your first experience with haiku, you might be surprised to learn that April 17th is National Haiku Poetry day. Supported by The Haiku Foundation it is *"a celebration of the genre of haiku"....whose origins date back a millennium in Japan; and more specifically, of English-language haiku, which has now been written for more than a century. ...the celebration of haiku occurs in the heart of the United States' celebration of National Poetry Month."* As well it should. As such, **The Hotel Haikus** would be a great addition in the celebration of this poetic art form!

CHECK-OUT

***

About the Authors

TS Hawkins is ecstatic to produce her second collection of short poems with fellow poet and Temple University Poetry as Performance alumni, T. McLean!

Since the fire of 2011, Hawkins has been expanding her artistic boundaries. She finished a **Puppets and Poets** residency in New York with Alphabet Arts. This program spring boarded Hawkins out of her poetry bubble to produce "poem as play" and learn the basic fundamentals of puppetry. Her piece *Seeking Silence* received rave reviews from the audience and program directors. She is looking forward to bringing the piece back to the stage for its Philadelphia premiere and its off-off Broadway debut in NYC. Finding solace in the New York poetry scene, Hawkins worked as a judge and coach for **Poetry Out Loud**; an educational organization where young poets recite classic poems in slam competition form. In her spare time, she tours and performs with her other works. Recently, she was featured in *Certain Circuits* magazine, *Third Sunday Blog Carnival*, a CD compilation by Drexel University, and Lady M Productions CD *Arts4TheCause*. Also, in April 2012, Hawkins released her sophomore poetry album *Running Still Water*!

A Temple University **Poetry as Performance** alum, she has taken her skills outside the classroom and into the world. Since 2007, she has written four publications titled *Sugar Lumps and Black Eye Blues*, *Confectionately Yours*, *Mahogany Nectar* and *Lil Blæk Book: All the Long Stories Short*. Next to be released is *Black Suga: diary of a troublesome teenager* and *Poetry Schmo-etry* which will be poetry collections for children and teens. It is with hope that they will follow in the latter books' successes in print and radio media. Selections from her books have been featured at: BAX, 107.9 WRNB, Verseadelphia, LP Spoken Word Tour, Brown Girl Radio: a Cure for the Common, Da Block, WRTI 90.1 FM, Studio Luna,

Improv Café, Temple University, PBGP, Aspire Arts, NBC 10, Moonstone: 100 Poets Reading, NateBrown Entertainment, The Liacouras Center, Tree House Books, The Bowery, Warmdaddy's, Jus Words, NJPAC, T Bar, Verbal Roots, The NAACP, The REC, Lyrical Playground, Lincoln University, The Pleazure Principle, Bar 13, Robin's Bookstore, umuvme Radio, First Person Arts, Drexel University, The RED Lounge for AIDS Awareness, Women's Ink, Lady M Events, 6B Lounge, The Painted Bride, So 4Real, Charis Books, American Family Theater National Touring Ensemble, Authors Under 30 Book Tour, First Person Arts and Dr. Sonia Sanchez Literacy Night just to name a few.

Currently, she is the Producer/Host for her own radio show and owner of **HawkEye Entertainment, page2stage LLC**. On the horizon, Hawkins will be debut her new band, **Meredith & The Moonshine**; an all women of color country/bluegrass ensemble!

For bookings and detailed information:
www.TSPoetics.com

T McLean was born in Teaneck, New Jersey on December 25th, 1986. He spent most of his formative years growing up in New York City where he discovered his two passions; theater and writing. Since kindergarten, he has always felt compelled to perform. After given his first role at age five as Grumpy in *Snow White*, he knew performing was indeed a pursuable calling.

McLean continued to act and perform throughout his childhood, but eventually began to execute his own original works. He began crafting short stories, articles, plays, and poetry where he oft found himself lost in a mystical world of his own musings; finding solace in the words he created on the page. He, looking to take his writing to the next level, got his poetry published. He began small, publishing first in his school newsletter and soon received accolades for his poems published in **Newsday**. Subsequently, he decided to take a small hiatus from writing to return to acting.

In 2005 he attended Temple University, where he studied Theater and Broadcasting. It was there, McLean learned how to web his two passions. As part of his theatrical curriculum, he took a myriad of acting and writing courses. But as semesters forged onward, he found a course that spoke to his precise need. **Poetry as Performance**, a class created and instructed by Dr. Kimmika Williams-Witherspoon, gave him the edge that he needed to stand out. Post-graduation, McLean went on to perform **off-Broadway**, in *Ma Rainey's Black Bottom*, *Roofless* and a variety of other productions. In 2010, he was named **#17** in **Curtains Up Top 25 Actors Under 25**. After such a successful dramatic stint, he decided to place greater emphasis on creating his own original works and bringing them to life on the stage.

McLean currently resides in New York City, where he continues to work in and around the arts. He continues to find new ways to blend his artistic desires to produce new forms of creative expression.

POEM GLOSSARY

***

Hawkins, TS

2, 7, 10, 14, 18, 20, 21, 22, 23, 24, 26, 27, 28, 30, 32, 33, 36, 37, 38, 40, 44, 45, 46, 48, 49, 50, 52, 53, 56, 57, 58, 59, 60, 63, 64, 66, 69, 71, 74, 75, 76, 77, 78, 79, 80, 81, 82, 83, 84, 87, 89, 90, 92, 93, 96, 97, 98, 100

McLean, T

1, 3, 4, 5, 6, 8, 9, 11, 12, 13, 15, 16, 17, 19, 25, 29, 31, 34, 35, 39, 41, 42, 43, 47, 51, 54, 61, 62, 65, 67, 68, 70, 72, 73, 85, 86, 88, 91, 94, 95, 99

Printed in the United States
By Bookmasters